This
Sprinkle of *Glitter*
diary belongs to

....

To Maddie, who not only organises
my whole life, but laughs at
my terrible jokes every day.

First published in 2016
by Faber & Faber, Bloomsbury House, 74–77 Great Russell Street, London WCIB 3DA
Designed and typeset by Faber & Faber Ltd
Printed in China

Clauses in the Banking and Financial Dealings Act allow the government to alter dates
at short notice.

A CIP record for this book is available from the British Library

ISBN 978-0-571-33043-0

MIX
Paper from
responsible sources
FSC® C005748

Sprinkle of Glitter

DIARY 2017

About me!

Aloha, Sprinklerinos!

Welcome to my Sprinkle of Glitter 2017 Diary!

As you may know, I'm Louise and I'm a Blogger, Vlogger, Author, Fashion Designer, Sister, Friend, Mother, Opportunity-Taker and Glitter-Sprinkler!

This diary is all about making the most of life and it's full of all the things I love to think about and do. I hope that it will make your life a little bit more sparkly, and that it'll help you make lots of extra-special memories along the way.

Don't forget — I'll be using the diary all year, too, and there are hashtags throughout to keep us in touch, so we can all have fun together in our special diary club.

Enjoy!

Lots of love,

Louise
xxx

- @SprinkleofGlitr
- sprinkleofglitter.blogspot.co.uk
- instagram.com/Sprinkleofglitr
- youtube.com/Sprinkleofglitter
- facebook.com/Sprinkleofglitter

About you!

 Name

....

Nicknames

....

 Phone number

....

 Email address

....

 Address

....

....

....

 Twitter handle

....

Instagram handle

....

YouTube name

....

Your favourites!

Blogs I like to read:

....

....

....

People on Twitter I enjoy following:

....

....

....

Vloggers I subscribe to:

....

....

....

Instagram accounts I ♥:

....

....

....

Suggestive sentences

I'm in love with ....

....

I can't stand the idea of ....

....

I dream of ....

....

I wish I could ....

....

....

I'm good at ....

....

My favourite thing about myself is ....

....

I'd like to try ....

....

I'd like to be better at ....

....

Annual Calendars 2017

JANUARY

M	T	W	T	F	S	S
26	27	28	29	30	31	1
2	3	4	5	6	7	8
9	10	11	12	13	14	15
16	17	18	19	20	21	22
23	24	25	26	27	28	29
30	31	1	2	3	4	5

FEBRUARY

M	T	W	T	F	S	S
30	31	1	2	3	4	5
6	7	8	9	10	11	12
13	14	15	16	17	18	19
20	21	22	23	24	25	26
27	28	1	2	3	4	5

MARCH

M	T	W	T	F	S	S
27	28	1	2	3	4	5
6	7	8	9	10	11	12
13	14	15	16	17	18	19
20	21	22	23	24	25	26
27	28	29	30	31	1	2

APRIL

M	T	W	T	F	S	S
27	28	29	30	31	1	2
3	4	5	6	7	8	9
10	11	12	13	14	15	16
17	18	19	20	21	22	23
24	25	26	27	28	29	30

MAY

M	T	W	T	F	S	S
1	2	3	4	5	6	7
8	9	10	11	12	13	14
15	16	17	18	19	20	21
22	23	24	25	26	27	28
29	30	31	1	2	3	4

JUNE

M	T	W	T	F	S	S
29	30	31	1	2	3	4
5	6	7	8	9	10	11
12	13	14	15	16	17	18
19	20	21	22	23	24	25
26	27	28	29	30	1	2

JULY

M	T	W	T	F	S	S
26	27	28	29	30	1	2
3	4	5	6	7	8	9
10	11	12	13	14	15	16
17	18	19	20	21	22	23
24	25	26	27	28	29	30
31	1	2	3	4	5	6

AUGUST

M	T	W	T	F	S	S
31	1	2	3	4	5	6
7	8	9	10	11	12	13
14	15	16	17	18	19	20
21	22	23	24	25	26	27
28	29	30	31	1	2	3

SEPTEMBER

M	T	W	T	F	S	S
28	29	30	31	1	2	3
4	5	6	7	8	9	10
11	12	13	14	15	16	17
18	19	20	21	22	23	24
25	26	27	28	29	30	1

OCTOBER

M	T	W	T	F	S	S
25	26	27	28	29	30	1
2	3	4	5	6	7	8
9	10	11	12	13	14	15
16	17	18	19	20	21	22
23	24	25	26	27	28	29
30	31	1	2	3	4	5

NOVEMBER

M	T	W	T	F	S	S
30	31	1	2	3	4	5
6	7	8	9	10	11	12
13	14	15	16	17	18	19
20	21	22	23	24	25	26
27	28	29	30	1	2	3

DECEMBER

M	T	W	T	F	S	S
27	28	29	30	1	2	3
4	5	6	7	8	9	10
11	12	13	14	15	16	17
18	19	20	21	22	23	24
25	26	27	28	29	30	31

2018

JANUARY
M	T	W	T	F	S	S
1	2	3	4	5	6	7
8	9	10	11	12	13	14
15	16	17	18	19	20	21
22	23	24	25	26	27	28
29	30	31	1	2	3	4

FEBRUARY
M	T	W	T	F	S	S
29	30	31	1	2	3	4
5	6	7	8	9	10	11
12	13	14	15	16	17	18
19	20	21	22	23	24	25
26	27	28	1	2	3	4

MARCH
M	T	W	T	F	S	S
26	27	28	1	2	3	4
5	6	7	8	9	10	11
12	13	14	15	16	17	18
19	20	21	22	23	24	25
26	27	28	29	30	31	1

APRIL
M	T	W	T	F	S	S
26	27	28	29	30	31	1
2	3	4	5	6	7	8
9	10	11	12	13	14	15
16	17	18	19	20	21	22
23	24	25	26	27	28	29
30	1	2	3	4	5	6

MAY
M	T	W	T	F	S	S
30	1	2	3	4	5	6
7	8	9	10	11	12	13
14	15	16	17	18	19	20
21	22	23	24	25	26	27
28	29	30	31	1	2	3

JUNE
M	T	W	T	F	S	S
28	29	30	31	1	2	3
4	5	6	7	8	9	10
11	12	13	14	15	16	17
18	19	20	21	22	23	24
25	26	27	28	29	30	1

JULY
M	T	W	T	F	S	S
25	26	27	28	29	30	1
2	3	4	5	6	7	8
9	10	11	12	13	14	15
16	17	18	19	20	21	22
23	24	25	26	27	28	29
30	31	1	2	3	4	5

AUGUST
M	T	W	T	F	S	S
30	31	1	2	3	4	5
6	7	8	9	10	11	12
13	14	15	16	17	18	19
20	21	22	23	24	25	26
27	28	29	30	31	1	2

SEPTEMBER
M	T	W	T	F	S	S
27	28	29	30	31	1	2
3	4	5	6	7	8	9
10	11	12	13	14	15	16
17	18	19	20	21	22	23
24	25	26	27	28	29	30

OCTOBER
M	T	W	T	F	S	S
1	2	3	4	5	6	7
8	9	10	11	12	13	14
15	16	17	18	19	20	21
22	23	24	25	26	27	28
29	30	31	1	2	3	4

NOVEMBER
M	T	W	T	F	S	S
29	30	31	1	2	3	4
5	6	7	8	9	10	11
12	13	14	15	16	17	18
19	20	21	22	23	24	25
26	27	28	29	30	1	2

DECEMBER
M	T	W	T	F	S	S
26	27	28	29	30	1	2
3	4	5	6	7	8	9
10	11	12	13	14	15	16
17	18	19	20	21	22	23
24	25	26	27	28	29	30
31	1	2	3	4	5	6

2019

JANUARY
M	T	W	T	F	S	S
30	1	2	3	4	5	6
7	8	9	10	11	12	13
14	15	16	17	18	19	20
21	22	23	24	25	26	27
28	29	30	31	1	2	3

FEBRUARY
M	T	W	T	F	S	S
28	29	30	31	1	2	3
4	5	6	7	8	9	10
11	12	13	14	15	16	17
18	19	20	21	22	23	24
25	26	27	28	1	2	3

MARCH
M	T	W	T	F	S	S
28	29	30	31	1	2	3
4	5	6	7	8	9	10
11	12	13	14	15	16	17
18	19	20	21	22	23	24
25	26	27	28	29	30	31

APRIL
M	T	W	T	F	S	S
1	2	3	4	5	6	7
8	9	10	11	12	13	14
15	16	17	18	19	20	21
22	23	24	25	26	27	28
29	30	1	2	3	4	5

MAY
M	T	W	T	F	S	S
30	31	1	2	3	4	5
6	7	8	9	10	11	12
13	14	15	16	17	18	19
20	21	22	23	24	25	26
27	28	29	30	31	1	2

JUNE
M	T	W	T	F	S	S
26	27	28	29	30	1	2
3	4	5	6	7	8	9
10	11	12	13	14	15	16
17	18	19	20	21	22	23
24	25	26	27	28	29	30

JULY
M	T	W	T	F	S	S
1	2	3	4	5	6	7
8	9	10	11	12	13	14
15	16	17	18	19	20	21
22	23	24	25	26	27	28
29	30	31	1	2	3	4

AUGUST
M	T	W	T	F	S	S
29	30	31	1	2	3	4
5	6	7	8	9	10	11
12	13	14	15	16	17	18
19	20	21	22	23	24	25
26	27	28	29	30	31	1

SEPTEMBER
M	T	W	T	F	S	S
26	27	28	29	30	31	1
2	3	4	5	6	7	8
9	10	11	12	13	14	15
16	17	18	19	20	21	22
23	24	25	26	27	28	29
30	1	2	3	4	5	6

OCTOBER
M	T	W	T	F	S	S
30	1	2	3	4	5	6
7	8	9	10	11	12	13
14	15	16	17	18	19	20
21	22	23	24	25	26	27
28	29	30	31	1	2	3

NOVEMBER
M	T	W	T	F	S	S
28	29	30	31	1	2	3
4	5	6	7	8	9	10
11	12	13	14	15	16	17
18	19	20	21	22	23	24
25	26	27	28	29	30	1

DECEMBER
M	T	W	T	F	S	S
26	27	28	29	30	31	1
2	3	4	5	6	7	8
9	10	11	12	13	14	15
16	17	18	19	20	21	22
23	24	25	26	27	28	29
30	31	1	2	3	4	5

A year in your world

What were you most proud of in 2016?

....

What were your biggest achievements?

....

What were your most cherished memories?

....

What do you hope for in 2017?

....

What would you like to change?

....

What would you like to do better?

....

26 Monday

27 Tuesday

28 Wednesday

29 Thursday

30 Friday

31 Saturday   NEW YEAR'S EVE

1 Sunday   NEW YEAR'S DAY
(UK, IRL, CA, AUS, ZA, NZ)

*Let's see the year out in style!
Party time!*

*Out with the old, in with the new!
Happy 2017!*

My 2016 New Year's resolutions were:

* Try new adventures
* Make more time for pampering
* Learn to dance
* Be a better friend
* Take Darcy on magical trips away

Write your top 5 New Year's resolutions here!

1 ....

2 ....

3 ....

4 ....

5 ....

#NewGlitterYear

2 *Monday* BANK HOLIDAY (UK, IRL, CA, USA, AUS, ZA, NZ)

3 *Tuesday*

4 *Wednesday*

5 *Thursday*

6 *Friday*

7 *Saturday*   8 *Sunday*

I hope the first week of Jan has been everything
you wanted it to be, Sprinklerinos!

MOTIVATION

We only regret the chances we didn't take.

9 Monday

10 Tuesday

11 Wednesday

12 Thursday

13 Friday

14 Saturday   15 Sunday

A new year, a new you!
Be brave and embrace life!

Tips!

Revamp your wardrobe for the coming year!

It's easy to feel short of cash after Christmas, but that's no reason not to dress to impress.

Here are my top tips for making your existing wardrobe feel fresh and exciting.

- Lay everything out on your bed and put together some outfits you've not tried before – you'll be surprised what goes together

- Take anything that doesn't fit you to a charity shop to create space

- Organise everything in colour order to make it easier to visualise an outfit

- Arrange your shoes at the bottom of your wardrobe so you can see which pair goes with what clothes

- Encourage your friends to do the same – you might even want to do a clothes swap at the end!

16 Monday

___

17 Tuesday

___

18 Wednesday

___

19 Thursday

___

Confidence is the best accessory!

20 Friday

___

21 Saturday   22 Sunday

Favourites!

The weather's often not great at this time of year, but that doesn't mean life can't be fun.

Here are my favourite things to do indoors:

- Take long bubble baths
- Watch my favourite vlogs
- Write notes/make cards for friends
- Eat yummy snacks – mmm, cheese and crackers!

What do you like to do?

#GlitterHibernate

23 Monday

24 Tuesday

25 Wednesday   BURNS NIGHT

Grab some tartan, Scottish Sprinklerinos!

26 Thursday   AUSTRALIA DAY (AUS)

Enjoy the celebrations, Aussie Sprinklerinos!

27 Friday

28 Saturday   29 Sunday

Curl up with a plate of cookies...

INGREDIENTS:

- 100g brown sugar
- 225g self-raising flour
- 125g unsalted butter
- 1 egg
- 200g chocolate chips
- 1½ tsp vanilla essence
- ½ tsp salt

INSTRUCTIONS:

1. Preheat the oven to 200°C.
2. Combine the butter and sugar in a large mixing bowl and mix until they are blended together.
3. Add the egg and vanilla essence.
4. Sieve the flour and the salt into the mixture, and mix until combined.
5. Add the chocolate chips and mix. (You can also swap some of these for nuts or other ingredients. Experiment!)
6. Cover a baking tray with baking paper.
7. Roll the dough into little balls, about 2cm wide.
8. Set them out on the tray, making sure not to put them too close together. (You'll have to do several batches to bake all your cookies.)
9. Put them in the oven for 7–10 minutes. Check them regularly, and take them out earlier rather than later if you like them a little gooey in the middle!

30 Monday

31 Tuesday

Long, dark evenings … the perfect excuse to treat yourself!

1 Wednesday

2 Thursday

3 Friday

4 Saturday

5 Sunday

Winter wonderland doodle

Be inspired by the outdoors!

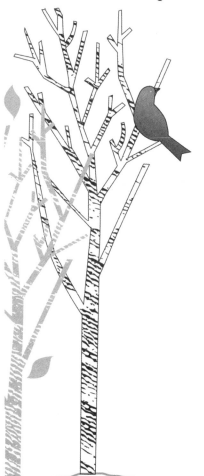

6 Monday   WAITANGI DAY (NZ)

Happy Waitangi Day, Kiwi Sprinklerinos!

7 Tuesday

8 Wednesday

9 Thursday

10 Friday

11 Saturday   12 Sunday

Make a Valentine's Day Card

Remember, it's the thought that counts! Make a card for a lover or a friend – or even someone in your family – to make them feel special this week.

#LASPAR

Maddie X

Love Glitter x

I lov

happy valentine's day

Share the love:
#GlitterLove

13 Monday

14 Tuesday ST VALENTINE'S DAY

♥ ♥ ♥ ♥ ♥ ♥ ♥ ♥ ♥ ♥ ♥ ♥ ♥ ♥ ♥

Love to all of YOU!

15 Wednesday

16 Thursday

17 Friday

18 Saturday   19 Sunday

Re-watch your favourite childhood movies

These are mine:

Three Men and a Little Lady

Mary Poppins

Now and Then

A Little Princess

What are yours?

⭐ ....

⭐ ....

⭐ ....

⭐ ....

20 Monday

---

21 Tuesday

---

22 Wednesday

Make the most of the cold … It's the perfect excuse for duvet snuggles!

23 Thursday

---

24 Friday

---

25 Saturday   26 Sunday

Pancake Day!

Here are my favourite toppings:

- ❖ Chocolate sauce
- ❖ Whipped cream
- ❖ Berries
- ❖ Edible glitter!

Don't forget to share your creations!

◄ #GlitterPancake

27 Monday

28 Tuesday   SHROVE TUESDAY

Happy Pancake Day! Nom, nom.

1 Wednesday   ASH WEDNESDAY, ST DAVID'S DAY

Happy day, Welsh Sprinklerinos!

2 Thursday

3 Friday

4 Saturday   5 Sunday

Make-up switch

Get a friend to do your make-up for you,
and then do hers in return. It's a great way
to try out a different look!

6 Monday

Change is good. Don't be afraid to try something new!

7 Tuesday

8 Wednesday

9 Thursday

10 Friday

11 Saturday　　　　12 Sunday

Make a lucky charm bracelet for St Patrick's Day

YOU WILL NEED:
(You can get all of these things from any good craft shop.)

- A chain and a clasp. You can buy these separately, but my trick is to buy a ready made bracelet. Then the hard bit is already done!
- Jump rings. These links connect your charms to your bracelet.
- Jewellery pliers.
- Lucky charms! A broken necklace? Old earrings or keyrings? Anything that feels lucky to you, Sprinklerinos!

1. Gather everything you want to attach to your bracelet, using your pliers to detach them from whatever they're currently connected to — but leave one ring or hoop on each charm.

2. Lay out your bracelet, and plan where you're going to put each charm. Try and space them out evenly.

3. Open up a jump ring with your pliers. Hook this through your charm's hoop, then one of the links on the bracelet chain, and squeeze it tightly closed. Make sure the jump ring is properly closed, or you risk your charms falling off!

4. Keep repeating step 3 until you've attached all of your charms. And voila! Remember, if you keep adding to it as you find more pretty things, your luck will just keep growing!

13 Monday

14 Tuesday

15 Wednesday

16 Thursday

17 Friday ST PATRICK'S DAY

Happy day, Irish Sprinklerinos!

18 Saturday

19 Sunday

Spring is here!

Why not rearrange your bedroom?
I find that a tidy room
makes for a tidy mind.

20 *Monday*

---

21 *Tuesday*

---

22 *Wednesday*

*Make sure you have space in your life for the new
exciting things that will come along this spring!*

---

23 *Thursday*

---

24 *Friday*

---

25 *Saturday*   26 *Sunday* MOTHER'S DAY (UK, IRL)

*Clocks go forward
(British Summer Time)*

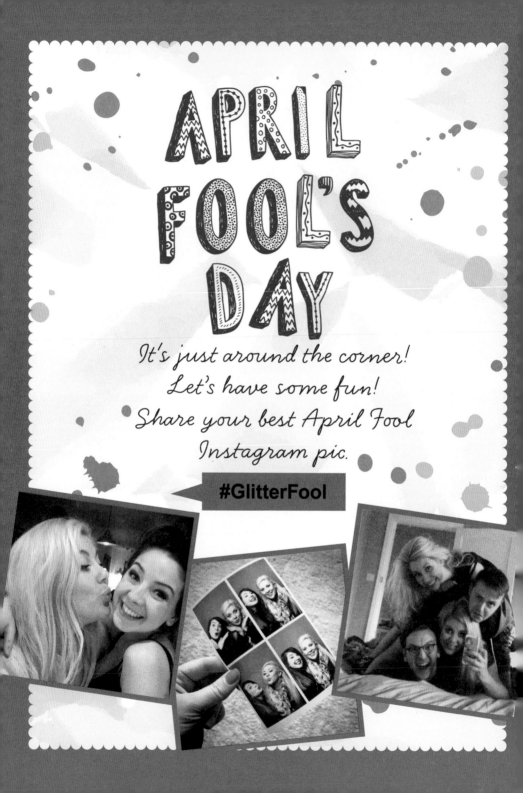

APRIL FOOL'S DAY

It's just around the corner!
Let's have some fun!
Share your best April Fool
Instagram pic.

#GlitterFool

27 Monday

28 Tuesday

Happy birthday, Zoe!

29 Wednesday

30 Thursday

31 Friday

1 Saturday   2 Sunday

April Fool's Day!
Unleash your playful side!

Happy 6th birthday,
Baby Glitter!

3 *Monday*

4 *Tuesday*

5 *Wednesday*

6 *Thursday*

Darcy is 6 today! How time flies!!

7 *Friday*

8 *Saturday*   9 *Sunday*

Decorate an Easter tree

YOU WILL NEED:

- Some stylish twigs or thin branches
- A vase
- Decorations!

WHAT TO DO:

1. Pop the twigs in your vase with a bit of water to keep them healthy.
2. Decorate with handpainted eggs, bunnies and birds.

10 *Monday*

11 *Tuesday*

12 *Wednesday*

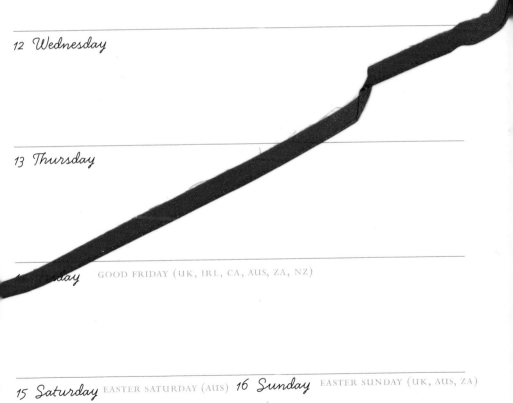

13 *Thursday*

...day   GOOD FRIDAY (UK, IRL, CA, AUS, ZA, NZ)

15 *Saturday* EASTER SATURDAY (AUS)   16 *Sunday* EASTER SUNDAY (UK, AUS, ZA)

Happy Easter, Sprinklerinos!

MOTIVATION
Let life surprise you!

17 *Monday* EASTER MONDAY (UK, IRL, CA, AUS, NZ), FAMILY DAY (ZA)

18 *Tuesday*

19 *Wednesday*

20 *Thursday*

21 *Friday*

22 *Saturday*

23 *Sunday* ST GEORGE'S DAY

Happy day, England!

It's my birthday!

And because it's all about ME (ha ha!) why not plan the perfect party?

Awesome playlist

Cocktails/ mocktails

Pick a party theme

Favourite snacks

Set a dress code

24 *Monday*

25 *Tuesday* ANZAC DAY (AUS, NZ)

26 *Wednesday*

27 *Thursday* FREEDOM DAY (ZA)

28 *Friday*

Happy birthday to ME!

29 *Saturday*

30 *Sunday*

Make your own garden!

I hope you're out enjoying the
spring flowers, Sprinklerinos!
If you're lucky enough to have a garden,
get out there and do some weeding.

YOU WILL NEED:

- Soil (you can buy this at a garden centre)
- A trowel (or a spoon will do!)
- A plant of your choice
- A terracotta pot – or an old pretty bowl!

WHAT TO DO:

1. Fill your pot or bowl with soil.
2. Using your trowel, make a hole in the middle of the soil that's wide enough to fit your plant in.
3. Pop your plant into the hole, and cover the roots with soil.
4. Pat the soil down fairly firmly – then give your plant a good glug of water to drink.

#GlitterGarden

1 *Monday*   EARLY MAY BANK HOLIDAY (UK), MAY DAY (IRL), WORKERS' DAY (ZA)

2 *Tuesday*

3 *Wednesday*

4 *Thursday*

5 *Friday*

There's nothing like some fresh air to brighten your day!

6 *Saturday*   7 *Sunday*

With summer just around the corner, grab your friends, some rugs and a picnic basket, and get out there and enjoy yourself!

8 *Monday*

9 *Tuesday*

10 *Wednesday*

Keep healthy, Sprinklerinos! A balanced
diet will help you feel great.

11 *Thursday*

12 *Friday*

13 *Saturday*

14 *Sunday*   MOTHER'S DAY (AUS, US)

It's fun to do something different – especially in the big outdoors.

Make a list (I love a list!)
of 5 new places to visit near you.

1 ....

2 ....

3 ....

4 ....

5 ....

15 Monday

16 Tuesday

17 Wednesday

18 Thursday

*Give out as many smiles as you can today.
You'll get plenty back!*

19 Friday

20 Saturday   21 Sunday

MOTIVATION

Their success is not your failure.

22 Monday   VICTORIA DAY (CA)

23 Tuesday

24 Wednesday

25 Thursday

26 Friday

It's Friday! Treat yourself to something nice today!

27 Saturday   START OF RAMADAN   28 Sunday

It might be a busy time for some
of you, at work or with exams.
Keep positive and take
a moment to think of all
the good things in your life.

Doodle the things that
make you happy:

29 *Monday*   SPRING BANK HOLIDAY (UK)

30 *Tuesday*

31 *Wednesday*

1 *Thursday*

Summer is coming ... Get excited, Sprinklerinos!

2 *Friday*

3 *Saturday*   4 *Sunday*

Get your skin ready for summer!

Here's my healthy summer skin routine:

- Exfoliate
- Moisturise
- Wear a high-factor sunscreen
- If you need a little help, why not try a bit of fake tan to give you a glow?

5 *Monday* JUNE BANK HOLIDAY (IRL), QUEEN'S BIRTHDAY HOLIDAY (NZ)

6 *Tuesday*

7 *Wednesday*

8 *Thursday*

Time to get those legs out! Summer dresses, anyone?

9 *Friday*

10 *Saturday*   11 *Sunday*

Get out into the garden with your friends and enjoy a jug of home-made lemonade.

INGREDIENTS:

(makes 8 servings)
- 10 lemons
- 300g sugar
- 3l water
- Magical-mystery extra ingredients!

INSTRUCTIONS:

1. Peel the rind off the lemons, and slice it into strips. Put the lemons themselves to one side.
2. Put all the rind in a large heatproof mixing bowl. Weigh out and add the sugar. Leave this bowl for an hour, so the sugar soaks up all the lemony juices.
3. Boil the water in a pan, and then pour it over the sugar and rind. Leave it for 20 minutes to cool down.
4. Squeeze the lemons into a separate bowl, then add the juice to the mixture, making sure you use a sieve. No pesky lemon pips!
5. Add any extra ingredients you fancy – raspberries? Mint? Get creative!
6. Mix well, pour into a jug, and put your lemonade in the fridge. Serve it later with some ice cubes, and a slice of something pretty on the side of the glass!

12 Monday

Is it time to get out the BBQ yet?

13 Tuesday

14 Wednesday

15 Thursday

16 Friday

17 Saturday

18 Sunday FATHER'S DAY (UK, IRL, US)

Make your daddy feel special today!

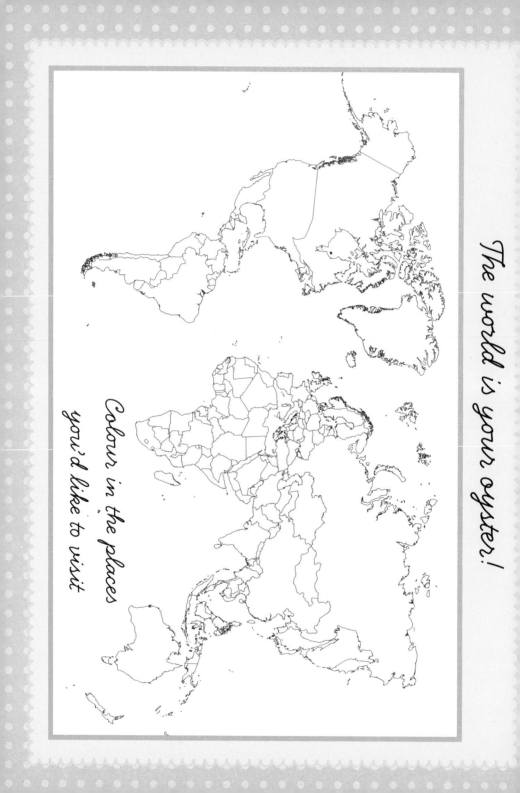

The world is your oyster!

Colour in the places you'd like to visit

19 Monday

20 Tuesday

21 Wednesday

The bigger the dreams, the further they'll take you . . .

22 Thursday

23 Friday

24 Saturday

25 Sunday   EID AL-FITR

Summer lovin'

I love spending time with my best
chummies in the sunshine.
Share a photo of you with yours!

#GlitterChummies

26 Monday

27 Tuesday

28 Wednesday

29 Thursday

30 Friday

1 Saturday   CANADA DAY (CA)   2 Sunday

*Happy day, Canadian
Sprinklerinos!*

MOTIVATION

Be your own kind of beautiful.

3 *Monday*

4 *Tuesday*   INDEPENDENCE DAY (US)

Happy Independence Day to my American Sprinklerinos!

5 *Wednesday*

6 *Thursday*

7 *Friday*

8 *Saturday*   9 *Sunday*

Plan your dream holiday

- ✏️ *Where would you go?*
- ✏️ *Which friends would you take?*
- ✏️ *Which books would you read?*
- ✏️ *What food would you eat?*
- ✏️ *What would you pack?*

10 Monday

There's always time for a spot of daydreaming!

11 Tuesday

12 Wednesday   BATTLE OF THE BOYNE HOLIDAY (NI)

13 Thursday

14 Friday

15 Saturday   16 Sunday

Sunsets can be beautiful at this time of year, and they're one of my favourite things. I find them so calming and soothing.

Photograph your best sunset and share it with me!

#GlitterSunset

17 *Monday*

*Keep your eyes open to all the beautiful things around you
— and make sure you have a camera handy!*

18 *Tuesday*

19 *Wednesday*

20 *Thursday*

21 *Friday*

22 *Saturday*   23 *Sunday*

Summer essentials checklist

🞷 Paint your toenails bright and fun colours

🞷 Dig out your favourite sun hat

🞷 Go to your local library or bookshop to find the perfect book to read in the sunshine

🞷 Make a summer playlist

24 *Monday*

---

25 *Tuesday*

---

26 *Wednesday*

---

27 *Thursday*

Summer is the perfect time for bright and bold colours.
Go for it, Sprinklerinos!

---

28 *Friday*

---

29 *Saturday*   30 *Sunday*

Summer ice pops

Ice lollies are super-easy to make. All you need are some lolly moulds, fruit juice or yoghurt, and anything else you fancy freezing in them. Pour your ingredients into the mould, put it in the freezer, and 4 hours later, you'll have some delicious ice pops!

IDEAS:

- Pineapple juice with banana slices
- Yoghurt with blueberries and honey
- Coconut milk with lime zest

31 Monday

1 Tuesday

2 Wednesday

3 Thursday

4 Friday

5 Saturday

6 Sunday

Everything tastes better in the sun.
Have as many meals outside as you can!

Yummy BBQ bananas!

This is a fun pudding recipe to try out after a BBQ!

YOU WILL NEED:

- One banana per person
- Chocolate – you'll need around one small bar per banana
- Aluminium foil
- BBQ tongs

INSTRUCTIONS:

1. Slit your banana lengthways down the middle, through the skin and into the banana – but don't cut all the way through!
2. Break up your chocolate into small pieces, and stuff it into the middle of the banana.
3. Wrap the banana up tightly in aluminium foil (so the chocolate doesn't escape!).
4. Carefully place your wrapped-up bananas in the embers of your BBQ coals – use the tongs!
5. After about 5 minutes, take the bananas out. If the chocolate is melted and the bananas are soft, you're done!

7 *Monday*   SUMMER BANK HOLIDAY (SCT, IRL)

8 *Tuesday*

9 *Wednesday*

10 *Thursday*

You are beautiful, Sprinklerinos — inside and out!

11 *Friday*

12 *Saturday*   13 *Sunday*

Tips!

My summer beauty survival guide

💜 Use a cute hairband to keep your hair off your face

💜 Keep eye make-up light and avoid creamy liners

💜 Opt for waterproof mascara for pool days

💜 Use plenty of conditioner on your hair after you've been in the sea

14 Monday

15 Tuesday

16 Wednesday

17 Thursday

A dip in the sea, anyone? I love getting my toes wet!

18 Friday

19 Saturday   20 Sunday

National Cuddle a Cat Week!
(OK, I'm not sure this has been signed off by the Queen, but it's my diary so I can make it so, right?)

Share your cat pics!

#GlitterCatCuddle

21 Monday

22 Tuesday

23 Wednesday

24 Thursday

25 Friday

26 Saturday

27 Sunday

As you probably know,
I LOVE stationery, and get very
excited about the amazing range
available at this time of year.
What would be in your
perfect pencil case?

Make a list:

━━ ....

━━ ....

━━ ....

━━ ....

━━ ....

28 *Monday*   SUMMER BANK HOLIDAY (UK, NOT SCOT)

29 *Tuesday*

30 *Wednesday*

31 *Thursday*   START OF EID AL-ADHA

1 *Friday*

September is the time for fresh starts.

2 *Saturday*

3 *Sunday*   FATHER'S DAY (AUS)

Back to school!

Ah, it's that time of year again, Sprinklerinos ...

Whether you're going back to school or uni, or just feel a bit glum that it's the end of summer, don't worry – and definitely don't stress! September is a time for new beginnings – embrace fresh starts and don't be afraid of the challenges that life can sometimes throw at you.

List five things you're looking forward to in September!

1.

2.

3.

4.

5.

#GlitterBackToSchool

4 *Monday* LABOUR DAY (CA)

---

5 *Tuesday*

---

6 *Wednesday*

---

7 *Thursday*

---

8 *Friday*

---

9 *Saturday*   10 *Sunday*

If you're missing the sun already, use some fake tan to give yourself a summery glow!

Take the time to connect
with old friends.
Go on – get in touch!
What's stopping you?

11 Monday

12 Tuesday

*I love making my home feel homely.
Do some nesting, Sprinklerinos!*

13 Wednesday

14 Thursday

15 Friday

16 Saturday

17 Sunday

MOTIVATION

Quit slackin' and make it happen!

18 Monday

19 Tuesday

20 Wednesday   ROSH HASHANAH

Work hard, but look after yourselves too, Sprinklerinos!

21 Thursday

22 Friday

23 Saturday   24 Sunday

Plan an autumn photoshoot with your friends. Autumn colours make a great backdrop.

Share your pics with me!

#SprinkleAutumn

25 Monday

26 Tuesday

27 Wednesday

Dig out those scarves and big knitted jumpers …
I love autumn clothes!

28 Thursday

29 Friday YOM KIPPUR

30 Saturday   1 Sunday

Autumnal table decoration

With so many pretty leaves around at this time of year, why don't you gather some up and make a seasonal table decoration?

Grab a bowl or vase and make your own arrangement – fill it with leaves you've collected, and add some flowers if you're feeling fancy.

You can add conkers or sycamore seeds too!

If you're feeling really crafty, why don't you make a harvest-themed decoration – use a pretty wicker basket, and fill it with miniature pumpkins and squashes.

2 Monday

*Bring a Thermos flask with you and you'll have
something warm and yummy to drink all day!*

3 Tuesday

4 Wednesday

5 Thursday

6 Friday

7 Saturday   8 Sunday

Warm yourself up with a hot drink! Here's my favourite recipe:

The ultimate hot chocolate

INGREDIENTS:

- 250ml double cream
- 250ml milk
- 200g dark chocolate

EXTRAS:

- Whippy cream
- Mini marshmallows
- Chocolate sprinkles

INSTRUCTIONS:

1. Break the chocolate into little pieces, and put them in a heatproof mixing bowl.
2. Put the cream and milk into a pan and heat slowly, until it's simmering, then take it off the heat. Don't let it boil!
3. Pour the cream and milk into the bowl with the chocolate, and stir well, until the chocolate has melted and mixed evenly into the liquid.
4. Use a ladle to pour the liquid into cups, and then get creative with the toppings! Marshmallows and squirty cream are the standards, but why not try adding something different? A chocolate flake? Raspberries? Anything goes!

9 Monday THANKSGIVING (CA)

Ask your friends about blogs they like.
You might find something new!

10 Tuesday

11 Wednesday

12 Thursday

13 Friday

14 Saturday

15 Sunday

Plan a bonfire party!

With Bonfire Night just two weeks away, why not plan a little party? Just remember – health and safety first, Sprinklerinos!

Build a bonfire

Yummy food

Drinks

Sparklers

Send invites

Cute hat and gloves

Fireworks

16 Monday

17 Tuesday

Keep moisturised, Sprinklerinos!
Cold weather can dry out your skin.

18 Wednesday

19 Thursday   DIWALI

20 Friday

21 Saturday   22 Sunday

It's nearly Halloween!

Post a pic of your Halloween costume.

#SpookyGlitter

23 *Monday* LABOUR DAY (NZ)

24 *Tuesday*

25 *Wednesday*

Watch some make-up tutorials for the best scary looks!

26 *Thursday*

27 *Friday*

28 *Saturday*   29 *Sunday*

Clocks go back
(End of British Summer Time)

Make your own toffee apples

It's Bonfire Night! Why don't you celebrate by making some traditional toffee apples?

YOU WILL NEED:

- 6 apples – try something soft, like a Red Delicious
- 300g Demerara sugar
- 3 tbsp golden syrup
- 25g unsalted butter
- 1½ tsp cider vinegar
- 75ml water
- Skewers – or lolly sticks!
- A cooking thermometer
- Baking paper

HOW TO MAKE:

1. Push your apples onto a skewer.
2. Melt all the sugar, syrup and butter together, then add the water.
3. Stir together, then slowly add in your vinegar.
4. Turn up the heat! Boil the mixture until it reaches 140°C.
5. VERY CAREFULLY dip your apples into the sugary syrup – use a spoon to coat them if your pan is too shallow.
6. Tip your apples upside down, and leave to cool on a plate or a baking tray that you've lined with baking paper.

30 Monday   OCTOBER BANK HOLIDAY (IRL)

31 Tuesday

Happy Halloween, my spooky Sprinklerinos!

1 Wednesday

2 Thursday

3 Friday

4 Saturday   5 Sunday

Bonfire Night!

Remembrance Sunday

Remember people who were special to you. Do something in their honour this week.

6 Monday

7 Tuesday

8 Wednesday

9 Thursday

10 Friday

11 Saturday

12 Sunday REMEMBRANCE SUNDAY

*Try to attend a local
Remembrance service today.*

Which winter coat is best for you?

Coats are one of my favourite things to wear because they make you feel so super snuggly! I like to find ones with furry linings to add extra cosiness, but it's always a good idea to have a 'special' coat in your wardrobe. Fit-and-flare styles go with most outfits and come in every colour of the rainbow. (I've got mint AND pink ones – what a surprise!)

The real trick is to make sure there is plenty of room for chunky jumpers, and big pockets to stash your gloves in!

13 Monday

14 Tuesday

15 Wednesday

16 Thursday

17 Friday

18 Saturday   19 Sunday

Compliment someone today.
You'll feel as good as they do!

MOTIVATION

Those who do not believe in magic will never find it.

20 Monday

21 Tuesday

22 Wednesday

23 Thursday   THANKSGIVING (US)

Happy Thanksgiving American Sprinklerinos!
Who do you want to say thank you to?

24 Friday

25 Saturday   26 Sunday

Christmas shopping list

Be prepared so you don't find gift-hunting
too stressful — no one likes to rush!

Who is the present for?	Ideas for presents

27 Monday

28 Tuesday

29 Wednesday

30 Thursday ST ANDREW'S DAY HOLIDAY (SCT)

1 Friday

And the countdown begins, Sprinklerinos!

2 Saturday   3 Sunday

Make your own snowflake decorations

YOU WILL NEED:

- White paper
- Scissors
- String

WHAT TO DO:

1. Start with a square piece of paper. (If you have A4 paper, trim it down to a square shape.)
2. Fold the paper in half along the diagonal.
3. Fold once more along the diagonal. (You should have a thin triangle now, one corner of which would be in the middle of the square if you opened it.)
4. Cut out little shapes and notches all along the edges of the paper. Make sure you leave some space between them. Don't leave too much blank space in the middle of the triangle though – if you can cut out a shape from the middle of it, do.
5. Open the square out. A snowflake!
6. Repeat, until you have lots of different snowflakes.
7. Tie string through one of the holes in each snowflake, and hang them up around your house!

4 Monday

5 Tuesday

6 Wednesday

7 Thursday

8 Friday

Look out for local Christmas markets.
I love to do my Christmas shopping there!

9 Saturday

10 Sunday

Have you got your
Christmas party
outfit sorted?
Share a photo!
I like lots of sparkles at
Christmas! Sequins ahoy!

#GlitterGlamour

11 *Monday*

12 *Tuesday*   START OF HANUKKAH

Sparkly eyeshadow, sparkly nail polish ...
this season is all about sparkles!

13 *Wednesday*

14 *Thursday*

15 *Friday*

16 *Saturday*
DAY OF RECONCILIATION (ZA)

17 *Sunday*

Christmas is NEXT WEEK and it's time to treat yourself. Why not plan a day out with friends or family?

Here are the sort of things I love to do at this time of year:

- Go ice skating
- See a panto at the theatre
- See the Christmas lights
- Find a friend and grab a hot chocolate in a cosy cafe

18 *Monday*

19 *Tuesday*

20 *Wednesday*

What's on top of your Christmas tree, my Sprinkle angels?

21 *Thursday*

22 *Friday*

23 *Saturday*

24 *Sunday*   CHRISTMAS EVE

Happy Christmas, Sprinklerinos!

I've recorded a special Christmas message just for you, my little diary chummies! Check out my YouTube channel on Christmas Day!

▶ YouTube /Sprinkleofglitter

25 Monday   CHRISTMAS DAY

Happy Christmas, Sprinklerinos!

26 Tuesday   BOXING DAY (UK, CA, AUS, NZ), DAY OF GOODWILL (ZA)

27 Wednesday

28 Thursday

29 Friday

30 Saturday

31 Sunday   NEW YEAR'S EVE

It's been nice knowing you, 2017 . . .

HAPPY NEW YEAR, SPRINKLERINOS!

Wow! What a year, Sprinklerinos!

I hope you enjoyed a year with my diary by your side!

Life can be a roller coaster! Although I'm sure 2017 was full of highs for you, perhaps there have been lows too. Take the time to be kind to each other, but also to be kind to yourself. Either way, remember that with a new day comes a fresh start and that nobody's perfect. And with the new year comes the freshest start of all!

Toodle pip, 2017 and WELCOME – 2018!
Lots of love,

Louise
xxx

- @SprinkleofGlitr
- sprinkleofglitter.blogspot.co.uk
- instagram.com/Sprinkleofglitr
- youtube.com/Sprinkleofglitter
- facebook.com/Sprinkleofglitter

NOTES

NOTES

NOTES

NOTES

NOTES

NOTES